Beliefs, Valu & Traditions

HINDUISM

SANATAN DHARMA

ANN LOVELACE & JOY WHITE

Heinemann

Heinemann Educational Publishers
Halley Court, Jordan Hill, Oxford OX2 8EJ
a division of Reed Educational & Professional
Publishing Ltd

MELBOURNE AUCKLAND FLORENCE PRAGUE
MADRID ATHENS SINGAPORE TOKYO SAO PAULO
CHICAGO PORTSMOUTH NH MEXICO IBADAN
GABORONE JOHANNESBURG KAMPALA NAIROBI

First Published 1997

00 99 98 97 96
10 9 8 7 6 5 4 3 2 1

**British Library Cataloguing in Publication
Data**
A catalogue record for this book is available from
the British Library
ISBN 0 435 302523

Designed and typeset by Artistix, Oxon
Illustrated by Artistix, Ed Dovey, Oxford
Illustrators, David Mostyn and Diana Bowles
Cover designed by Threefold Design
Printed and bound in Great Britain by Bath Press
Colourbooks, Glasgow

Acknowledgments

This book is dedicated to Indryesha and Rasamandala
Das of ISKCON in recognition for the support and
inspiration they give to countless pupils, students and
teachers.

The authors would like to thank the following people for
their invaluable help and advice: Michelle Golden,
Kalpna Patel, Bob Potter, Narinda Sharman and Ben
Gamadia of Navjivan, Leicester, Ranchor Prime and
Friends of Vrindavan, Mrs Gosht of Swaminarayan
School, Mr Patel of the Swaminarayan Temple, Robert
Vint of REEP, Mr Shah of Asian Funeral Service, Mr
Surur Hoda of The Gandhi Foundation, Alistair Christie
and Alex Gray of Heinemann Educational, Jennifer
Johnson, photo researcher, V. P. (Hemant) Kanitkar, and
members of:

● Food for Life
● The National Hindu Students Association
● Shree Radha Krishna Cultural Centre, Norwood
● ISKCON Educational Services.

In particular, very special thanks are due to
Rasamandala Das for the many hours of work and
scholarship he gave so willingly to help the authors
bring this book to fruition.

The publishers would like to thank the following for
the copyright material reproduced in this book:
Tom Coop for the cartoon p. 5; the illustration by
Sanjay Sinha on p.12 was reprinted with permission
from *A World in Our Hands* by Peace Child Charitable
Trust, copyright © 1995. ($15.95, Tricycle Press,
800-841-BOOK); Friends of Vrindavan for the logo
and Sunder Art Sales for the postcard picture on
p. 16; Bhakdivedanta Manor Cow Protection Project
for the extracts from 'Adopt your own cow' on p. 20;
Eastern Eye for the articles on pp. 21, 39 and 45 and
the quotation from Meera Syal on p. 39; the extract
from the *Sunday Times* on p. 23 is © Times
Newspapers Ltd, 1996; the logo of Hare Krishna –
Food for Life on p. 24 and the cartoon on p. 33 were
reproduced courtesy of the International Society for
Krishna Consciousness; Britstock IFA for the 'love
safely' picture on p. 26; *Hinduism Today* for the
cartoon on p. 28; the Swaminarayan School, 260
Brebtfield Road, Neasden, London NW10 8HE, tel
0181-965 8381, for the extract from their brochure
on p. 35; the extract from *A Suitable Boy* by Vikram
Seth on p. 37 is copyright © Vikram Seth 1993;
National Hindu Students' Forum (UK) for their logo
on p. 39; the extract of a dialogue between an atheist
and a Hindu on p. 42 and the quote by Richard
Branson on p. 44 from *Swaminarayan Bliss*, Oct-Nov
1995 (pp. 9, 120), a monthly magazine of the
Swaminarayan Movement, published by Swaminarayan
Aksharpith, Amdavad, India 38004; extract from
article by Ruth Gledhill from *The Times* on p. 44 is
© Times Newspapers Ltd, 1995; Bloomsbury
Publishing Plc for the quotation from *Dark Horse –
The Secret Life of George Harrison* on p. 48; Gandhi
Book House for the postcard picture, titled 'Gandhi
as I see him', on p. 50; the Gandhi Foundation for
the logo on p. 50; the Concordia Project and Saatchi
and Saatchi for the brochure material on p. 53;
Hinduism Today for the cartoon and SEWA
International for the logo on p. 55; the plate on p. 56
was reproduced courtesy of Swaminarayan Aksharpith,
publication on Lord Swaminarayan's personality
exhibited at Akshardam, India; the lyrics from 'Beware
of Darkness' by George Harrison on p. 56 are © 1970
Harrisongs Ltd; City Cruises for the logo on p. 60;
Daily Mail and *Hinduism Today* for the articles on
p. 61; Ford of Europe, Inc. for the logo of Jaguar
cars on p. 61.

The publishers would like to thank the following for
permission to reproduce photographs:
p. 10 Michael Neveux/Westlight; p. 13 (left) Natural
History Museum, London, (right) Heather Angel;
p. 14 Motor Presse International/Zefa; p. 16 Friends
of Vrindavan; p. 17 Associated Press; p. 18 Dudley
Zoo; p. 19 Carlos Freire/Hutchison Library; p. 22
Marcello Bertinetti; p. 23 (top) Tom Coop; p. 24 (top)
Ruth Tayler, (bottom) Atul and Jogi Images; p. 25 Atul
and Jogi Images; p. 26 (top) Britstock-IFA/Haga,
(bottom) Savita Kirloskar/Reuters/Popperfoto; p. 30
Gayatri Wedding Services; p. 31 Mohamed
Ansar/Impact; p. 32 (left) *Eastern Eye*, (right) David
Hanover/Tony Stone Images; p. 34 Yamaraja
Dasa/Bhaktivedama Book Trust International; p. 35
Swaminarayan Temple; p. 36 (top) Michelle Golden;
p. 38 Associated Press; p. 43 Swaminarayan School;
p. 44 (top) Swaminarayan Temple, (bottom) *Eastern
Eye*; p. 48 A. Rowlands; p. 49 *Hinduism Today*; p. 50
Gandhi Foundation; p. 51 Nils Jorgensen/Rex
Features; p. 52 Roderick Johnson/ Panos; p. 54 (top)
Comstock Photo Library, (bottom) Eleanor Bentall;
p. 55 *Eastern Eye*; p. 58 Michelle Golden; p. 60 City
Cruises; p. 61 Jaguar Cars; p. 62 Zefa; p. 63
Swaminarayan Temple.

Contents

Notes for teachers

Beliefs, Values & Traditions: Hinduism is designed for Key Stage 4 students doing a GCSE Religious Education (Short Course) or a general non-examination course. It follows a similar format to its predecessor *Beliefs, Values & Traditions*, which focuses on Christianity, Islam and Judaism.

This short book concentrates on how beliefs, values and traditions affect the lifestyle of Hindus in Britain today. It can only begin to reflect the wealth of philosophy and practice found within Hinduism. For this reason we would particularly recommend inviting Hindu speakers to talk to classes. This can be particularly useful in exploring the great diversity of belief, particularly evident in discussing the nature of God.

The SCAA glossary has been used as the basis for spellings and definitions. Pupils who have knowledge of Sanskrit may be used to different spellings, especially for festivals and rites of passage. The study of Hinduism has sometimes suffered from an erroneous use of terminology. At Key Stages 3 and 4, it can still be necessary to correct pupils' misconceptions regarding 'idol worship' and the original meaning of the swastika.

How it fits in with the GCSE Religious Education (Short Course)

- Its subject content supports many of the syllabuses.
- It follows the examination criteria.
- It uses the SCAA glossary spellings and definitions of terms.
- It contains GCSE-type questions with a mark allocation guide.
- It provides scope for evaluation through discussion questions.

How it meets the needs of non-examination courses

- It uses stimulating material about relevant issues today.
- It follows the two SCAA Model Syllabus Attainment Targets – Learning about religions and Learning from religion.
- It allows differentiation through a variety of stimuli and questions.
- It consolidates learning in earlier Key Stages.

Some useful addresses of agencies referred to within the book:

Friends of Vrindavan
Environ
Parkfield
Western Park
Hinckley Road
Leicester LE3 6HX

ISKCON Educational Services
Bhaktivedanta Manor
Hilfield Lane
Aldenham
Watford
Hertfordshire WD2 8EZ

Age Concern (Navjivan)
Clarence House
46 Humberstone Gate
Leicester LE1 3PJ

National Hindu Students Forum (NHSF)
46-48 Loughborough Road
Leicester LE4 5LD

Swaminarayan Temple
Brentford Road
Neasden
London NW10 8HD

Notes for students

Welcome to *Beliefs, Values & Traditions: Hinduism*, which is written to help you discover that religion is not just about the past, but it is also very much alive and part of today's world. Whether you are studying for GCSE or doing general RE, you will find that this book contains a great deal about the important issues that face all people at different stages of their lives. Your teacher will help you to get the most out of the book. You might find it helpful to read the notes on the opposite page.

Practical help

- **Do** take time if you can to explore the diversity of beliefs, values and traditions within Hinduism.
- **Do** look in magazines for articles and features about the issues you are studying. Bring them to school for discussion or for display. Keep a folder of them.
- **Do** write off to relevant organizations. The information you will receive will support your work and help you with your creative assignments. (See list on page 4).
- **Do** try to visit various Hindu places of worship including mandirs and home shrines.
- **Do** ask friends and family who are going abroad to bring you back pictures and information. Hinduism is practised in many countries around the world.
- **Do** take a camera when you go away.

How to answer questions

- **RE**fer to the number in brackets after each question.
- **RE**fer to the Fact files, features and pictures in the section.
- **RE**fer to all the introduction sections.
- **RE**fer to the index.
- **RE**fer to your teacher.

And finally ...

- **Don't** be blinkered about religion. Keep an open mind and respect people's views, even if you don't share them. Many of the world's problems are caused by intolerance brought about through lack of knowledge and understanding. When you leave school you will be constantly meeting and mixing with people whose beliefs, values and traditions may be different from your own.

  But to some questions there are no answers.

Why did those all-night revision sessions seem such a good idea at the time?

Why doesn't even your favourite mascot guarantee the topics you've revised come up?

Why is some bright spark on his third sheet of paper when you've hardly started?

Why do some invigilators insist on eating garlic the night before?

Introduction to Hinduism

Sanatan Dharma

Hinduism is the name most often used to describe the faith and culture that is followed by many millions of people around the world. It originated in India nearly 5000 years ago. Many Hindus today, however, prefer to use the name **Sanatan Dharma**, which can be translated as the 'eternal laws of nature'. They see it as a fitting description for what is more than just a religion, but a way of life based on timeless and universal principles valid for all time and in all places.

Unity in diversity

Unlike most other religions, Hinduism has no one founder, no single scripture nor a unified set of teachings. It has many writings and consists of a wide variety of beliefs and practices all handed down over the centuries. It acknowledges that there are many paths to the truth and has a tolerant attitude to other faiths. Hindus do not believe it is right to try to convert people or impose their religion on others. Despite its breadth and diversity, it also has a unity and harmony owing to certain key beliefs that underpin it and give it its special identity.

God

Hindus believe in one God who can be understood in many ways. There are two main philosophies concerning the nature of God. **Advaita** (monism) teaches that the Supreme is an impersonal energy and equates God, the soul and matter. **Dvaita** (dualism) refers to belief in a personal God, who is distinguished from the soul and matter.

The many gods and goddesses worshipped by Hindus represent different aspects and forms of the one supreme God, **Brahman**.

Dharma

Dharma is an all-embracing term that is central to Hindu beliefs. It refers to the natural law and it is also used to describe duty, codes of conduct and the practice of religion itself. Each **ashrama** (stage of life) and **varna** (section of society) has its own dharma, or specific duties.

The cycle of life

Hindus believe that life is a continuous cycle of birth, death and rebirth. This is known as **samsara**. The **atman** (soul) perpetually moves through a series of lives in different species. This process of **transmigration** is hoped eventually to lead to **moksha**, a state of salvation and freedom in union with God. Hinduism teaches that a person's destiny is dependent on their **karma**. This is the law of cause and effect which states that all actions reap corresponding results. Hindus believe that whatever they do affects their future, in this life and in lives to come. They consider that performing one's dharma with no expectation of personal reward will bring one nearer to the ultimate liberation of moksha. This is a form of **yoga** by which the mind and body are trained to focus attention on God. There are many different types of yoga.

Sacred writings

Hindu scriptures fall into two main categories. The **Shrutis** refer to 'what is heard' and are believed to contain eternal truths. They include the four **Vedas**, which are the oldest scriptures and written in **Sanskrit** (a language regarded by Hindus as sacred). They contain rituals and **mantras** (hymns and prayers) for use in worship. The **Upanishads** also form part of the Shrutis. These consist of philosophical discussions between pupils and their **gurus** (spiritual teachers). The **Smritis** refer to 'what is remembered'.

These scriptures include the epics of the **Mahabharata** and the **Ramayana**, and the stories known as the **Puranas**. The **Bhagavad Gita** (the Song of the Lord) is contained in the Mahabharata. This is the most popular and important of the Hindu scriptures. It is a dialogue between Prince Arjuna and **Krishna** (a popular Hindu deity) and contains many important spiritual teachings.

Worship

Hindus worship at home using a home shrine and at the **mandir** (temple). The term generally used for worship is **puja**. During puja, offerings of food are made and mantras are recited to the **murti** (image) on whom devotion is focused.

The **arti** is a welcoming ceremony performed at home and in the mandir. It is often accompanied by the beating of a gong, by **bhajan** (devotional hymns) or by **kirtan** (repeating mantras to music).

There is a large number of Hindu festivals. The one most widely celebrated is **Divali**, often referred to as the Festival of Lights. For many Hindus, the festival marks the new financial year.

Other major festivals include **Janmashtami**, in August, when Krishna's birthday is celebrated, and **Holi**, in March, when bonfires are lit as a reminder of how Prince Prahlada was protected from burning by **Vishnu** (a Hindu diety).

Pilgrimage

Yatra (pilgrimage) is an important duty for many Hindus. Most of the places they visit are in India. These include **Varnasi**, on the **Ganga** (the River Ganges), which is considered the most sacred place, and the town of **Vrindavan**, where Krishna lived as a child.

Hindu society

Hindu teachings divide society into four **varnas** (sections in society), according to the role for which people are best fitted. These are:
- **brahmins** (priests and teachers)
- **kshatriyas** (soldiers and rulers)
- **vaishyas** (merchants and farmers), and
- **shudras** (labourers and craftsmen).

The teachings later incorporated sub-divisions called **jati**, which categorized people by birth rather than according to talent and personal qualities. This became the caste system.

A Hindu's life is separated into four distinct ashramas (stages), each with its own rituals and dharmas. These are:
- **brahmacharya** (student)
- **grihastha** (householder)
- **vanaprastha** (retirement), and
- **sannyasa** (renunciation).

This way of life is often called **varna-ashrama-dharma** and forms the basis of the Hindu social system.

There are also sixteen life-cycle rituals, the **samskars**. The most widely observed are those connected with birth, marriage and death.

Symbols

Many aspects and attributes of Hindu dieties can be seen through the symbols associated with them. For instance, **Lakshmi** is connected with bringing good fortune. She is represented standing on a lotus flower resting on water. As the lotus grows out of the mud it is a reminder of how it is possible for good to rise out of evil.

The **swastika**, with its arms extended to four corners, is often used to symbolize the changing world around the fixed, unchanging centre of God. It is used as a symbol of good fortune during a wedding ceremony.

Symbols also have an important role in worship. The **shankha** (conch shell) is often blown in the arti ceremony. Its spiral shape, which comes from one point, reminds Hindus that all **creation** stems from one God. Its sound represents the sacred **Aum** (or OM), which is the most important of all Hindu symbols. This is considered to be the first sound at the start of creation. It is uttered at the beginning and end of many mantras and for many Hindus it represents God himself. The symbol of Aum is sometimes included in **yantras**. These are geometric figures which, like mandalas, are used as aids to meditation.

The nature of God

'There is only one God, who resides deep inside all objects and beings. He is everywhere and the inner self of all.'
(Svetashvatara Upanishad 6:11)

The words in the quote above sum up the basis of what most Hindus believe about the nature of the Supreme Being known as Brahman. He is unlimited, the source and power of all life (omnipotent) and is all-knowing (omniscient). Hindus also describe Brahman as the ultimate reality which pervades the universe and is within everything (omnipresent). The atman (real self or soul) in all living things is considered to be a tiny fragment of Brahman and is eternal. Many Hindus believe that when they reach moksha (their final liberation), they will be reunited with God.

The universe is constantly going through the pattern of birth, growth and death. The three most important functions of God within this world relate to this continuous cycle of life. These three have corresponding deities known together as the **trimurti** and are represented by **Brahma** (not to be confused with Brahman) as the creator, Vishnu the preserver and **Shiva** the destroyer. The power

Shiva

and energy used to perform these functions is called **Shakti** and is seen in female form. Shakti is often thought of as the Divine Mother. The trimurti are believed to control the three **gunas** (qualities) of **sattva** (goodness), **rajas** (passion) and **tamas** (ignorance) which permeate and regulate all matter.

Hindus can be divided into three kinds of worshippers. Followers of Vishnu are known as **Vaishnavas**. Those worshipping Shiva are called **Shaivites**. The third group are the **Shaktas** who worship God in the form 0f Shakti. Some Hindus believe that at times of crisis these deities have descended into this world in various forms (**avatars**). Most popular and widely worshipped are **Rama** and Krishna, two of the avatars or incarnations of Vishnu. The last of Vishnu's avatars to appear on earth was the **Buddha** and it is thought that the tenth, **Kalki**, is yet to come.

In addition to the trimurti, there are many other deities who reflect different aspects of God. Many of them represent powers of nature such as **Varuna**, the god of water, and **Agni**, the god of fire. **Ganesha** represents the power to remove obstacles and is often worshipped by those embarking on a new or difficult stage in life. **Saraswati**, the goddess of learning, shows the power of knowledge and is often prayed to by students. Lakshmi, the goddess of good fortune, is particularly associated with the festival of Divali which begins the new financial year for Hindus.

Lakshmi

When Hindus worship, they often focus on their deities through a murti (image). Some Hindus are impersonalists and consider the Supreme as impersonal and so believe the various deities equally represent that all-pervading spirit. Other Hindus are personalists and believe the Supreme can also be represented through a particular deity, e.g. Krishna. For them other deities may have a lesser status. Whatever their point of view the different deities either directly or indirectly represent God. Hindus will often have their own Ishta-dev (chosen deity) who is the particular object of their devotions. Mandirs (temples) and home shrines contain murtis and these will be the main focus of public and private worship.

Children learn about the deities from an early age through being told stories about them from the sacred texts. These are often acted out in dramatic presentations or through dance, particularly at festival times.

Morality

Hindus' belief in karma (the law of cause and effect) influences them in the way they conduct their lives. They are aware that any wrong action not only harms others but themselves too and delays the time when they reach their ultimate goal of moksha (liberation). Hindus believe that God has given them free will and that they are individually answerable to Him for all their thoughts and actions. They are taught that their freedom should be balanced with responsibility.

'I hold both right and responsibility in my hand.'
(Rig Veda 1:168:3)

Hindu morality is based on a particular attitude to life in which it is considered important to live in harmony with nature. Many develop a code of conduct to limit selfishness, which could destroy the whole balance of nature. Any action or behaviour that goes against the natural order and that places faith solely in the material world is considered to be morally wrong.

Hindus often consider the world to be **maya** (illusory) because even though it appears to be real or permanent, it doesn't actually endure. Therefore, it is wrong to place too much reliance on it or the temporary pleasures it promises. Many of the sacred writings provide Hindus with guidelines on how they should conduct their lives.

Yamas (the five abstentions)

Yama means 'control' and the five yamas refer to an important code of morality based on refraining from certain wrong attitudes and actions associated with anger, lying, theft, lust and greed.

Niyamas (the five observances)

The niyamas set out positive steps for leading a good life. These include purity, contentment, patience, faith and devotion.

The niyamas are part of the **Ashtanga Yoga**, an eight-fold path of self-discipline, which teaches that yoga is an important way of learning to control the cravings and temptations that come into a person's mind. Unless these can be overcome, a person is unable to know the difference between good and bad. Each of the eight steps shows how the mind can be drawn away from selfish thoughts and directed towards God.

Dharma Shastras (law codes)

Dharma shastras are the ancient law codes of Hinduism. The best known of them is the **Manu Smriti** named after the law giver, Manu. The codes of Manu contain teachings on every aspect of moral and social behaviour. This involves all areas of life from the ethics of war to social etiquette and hygiene. It also contains the dharmas (duties) for each of life's four ashramas (stages), setting out rules of responsibility within relationships such as with the guru (spiritual leader) or within marriage.

Puranas

These are part of the Smriti texts and contain stories with a moral message, so providing another way of conveying morality and religious principles.

Spiritual teachers

Many Hindus are helped in their understanding of how they should conduct their lives by gurus (spiritual teachers). These may be priests giving personal guidance or famous **acharyas** (spiritual teachers) from the past and present who have set examples for others to follow.

The Sanctity of life

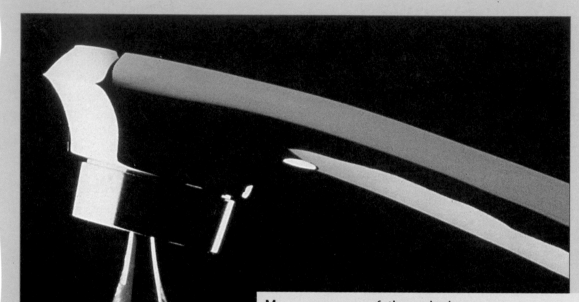

Many years ago a father asked
his son to pour some salt into
water. He did so and the next day he
was told to take it out again. Of course
this was impossible as the salt had dissolved.
But he knew that the salt was there because every
part of the water tasted of it even though it could
not be seen. 'This is like the soul,' said the father.
'It is within the body even though it is impossible to see it.'

(adapted from *Chandogya Upanishad 1:13 1–3*)

Get talking

- What things about a person do you know are true even though they cannot be seen?
- In what ways are people different from other forms of life?

Life is like a circle going round and round. One thing connected to another. Life is like a chain every day, every minute linked to one another, hook by hook. Life is like water flowing from second to second. From lakes to streams, streams to rivers and finally to the great ocean. We are all connected in the great circle of life, all humans, birds and animals.

(Bhav Mistry)

Creative assignment

Using a circle shape, show some of the ways in which people depend both on each other and on the rest of creation.

Hindus believe everything that lives and grows is interconnected. Where there is life or consciousness it is due to the presence of the atman (real self or soul). Hindus consider they *are* the soul but have a material body. At death, this soul enters another body or form.

'As a person puts on new garments, giving up old ones, the soul similarly accepts new material bodies, giving up the old and useless ones'. (Bhagavad Gita 2:22).

Hindus consider life to be sacred and worthy of the highest respect. This influences them when they are faced with the challenging decisions that need to be made about life and death issues (e.g. abortion, euthanasia).

This respect for life is also reflected in the Hindu namaste greeting.

'With all the power of my arms,
With all the intelligence of my mind,
With all the love of my heart,
I pay due respect to you, the soul within.'

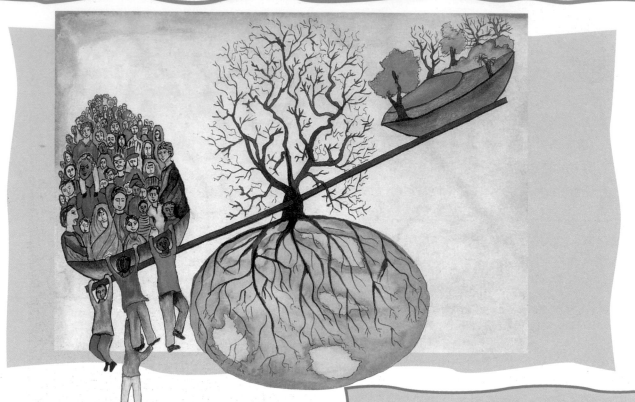

Upsetting the balance

Many people, like the artist of the picture, are deeply concerned about the misuse of the world's environment. Forests and animals are disappearing at alarming rates. Many rivers and even the air we breathe have become dangerously polluted. Humans have always lived by using nature's resources. Today, however, we are suffering the damaging effects of too much being taken from the environment and not enough being done in return to protect it.

 Get talking

- In what ways have human actions upset the natural balance of the world?

- What examples can you give of what 'selfless acts' might be?

Fact file

Hinduism teaches harmony with nature. Hindus are aware of how much humans depend on the environment for all their needs and how important it is not to upset the natural balance of creation (see page 7). According to the law of karma (see page 9) the more people use the earth's resources for their own ends, the more scarce these resources become. Hindus believe that nature's gifts all come from God. The sun is sometimes referred to as 'the eye of God'. The colour saffron is often used by Hindus to represent the sun's life-giving glow and acts as a reminder of the power of God.

Obeying God's laws by living unselfishly not only keeps the natural balance but is a repayment for the gifts that have been received.

'But anyone who enjoys these gifts without offering selfless acts in return is certainly a thief.' (Bhagavad Gita 3:12)

Seed from the banyan tree

Sanjay was about to do his homework as his mother prepared to do some sewing. 'Do you want me to help you thread that needle?' Sanjay asked as his mother struggled with it.

'I think my eyes need testing again,' she replied, handing him the needle and thread. 'I was just reminded of the story of the shoemaker and the banyan tree.'

Sanjay was puzzled, wondering what the connection was. But he knew he would soon find out. It meant another story from his mother's never-ending supply. 'Is there something special about a banyan tree? They seem to come into a lot of stories,' he asked.

'It's certainly very different,' said his mother. 'It has a massive trunk and from its branches, lots of smaller branches hang down to the ground and give out fresh roots.'

'So I suppose you're reminded of this shoemaker because he was mending shoes and you're mending socks!'

'Not even close,' laughed his mother. 'The story goes that a poor shoemaker was working under the shade of the banyan tree when he was visited by the famous teacher, Narada, who was a great devotee of Vishnu. Anyway, Narada invited the shoemaker to ask a question. The cobbler was always thinking of the Lord and therefore he asked, "What was Vishnu doing when you last saw him?" Vishnu knew the cobbler would ask this question and had already prepared Narada to say, "He was threading an elephant through the eye of a needle." The shoemaker was surprised but responded with a laugh, saying, "Well, only Vishnu could do that!"

'Narada expressed amazement that the shoemaker had believed his reply. "Why not?" replied the shoemaker. "He can do everything else. He can make the wind blow and the sun shine. Nothing is impossible."

'With that he bent down and picked up a seed from the banyan tree. "If Vishnu can squeeze a whole tree into a seed this size, surely he can thread an elephant through the eye of a needle."

'Narada realised that the cobbler, though poor and lowly by profession, possessed the wisdom to see God's hand in everything.'

A banyan tree

 **Get talking**

- What stories or fables have you read or been told that have been important to you?

Recall and explain

1 Why was Narada surprised at the cobbler's response? **(2)**

2 Explain why Hindus consider Vishnu to be so special. **(2)**

3 Explain why Hindus think it is wrong to 'upset the balance' of nature. **(6)**

'If there is only one tree full of flowers and fruits in a village, that place becomes worthy of respect.'
(Mahabharata)

Patient protector
Of living things,
Resting place
For weary wings.
Source of building,
Fuel to burn,
Paper for books
From which we learn.
Your masterful roots
The soil sustains
So it won't wash away
In the powerful rains.
As I sit in the glade
Under shade you have made,
I see the rhythm
Of life displayed.
From above and beneath
Your sturdy girth,
You are the lungs
And heart of the earth.

Creative assignment

Using the title 'Trees For Life' or 'Touch Wood', write a sketch or make up a cartoon that highlights the importance of trees in Hinduism.

The tree has a very special place in Hinduism. It is seen as the most important example of plant life. Many Hindus consider that like all living things, the tree has a soul (atman) which is rotating in the cycle of repeated birth and death.

Respect for trees has led Hindus both past and present to dedicated and brave actions. Examples include the **Chipko Movement** (see page 52), the Friends of Vrindavan Project (see page 16).

ig tree: used in some Hindu writings as a symbol of creation. It is sometimes shown upside down with the root above and three main stems coming down towards the earth. These represent Brahma (the creator), Shiva (the destroyer) and Vishnu (the preserver). Spreading from these, the branches represent other gods and goddesses such as Lakshmi and Ganesha.

ffering: a leaf from the tulsi bush, special to Krishna, is offered during puja by some Hindus (see page 37). The leaf is also used in death rituals (see page 58). Wood from the tulsi bush is used in making **malas** (beads used during meditation).

etreat: those who were preparing to become **sadhus** (priests) would often go to the forest to meditate. Many teachers of the holy scriptures led simple lives in the forest. They would sit beneath trees both to give and hear teaching. The Buddha (see page 8) received his Enlightenment (knowledge) under the bodhi tree.

ntrances to many mandirs (temples) have carvings of trees to remind worshippers of their importance. They can be seen, too, in the background of paintings of many Hindu deities (see page 16).

ingle banyan tree: Krishna, in the Bhagavad Gita, compares the material world with this vast tree. It is like a miniature forest and is home to many creatures. It is a reminder of the earth, which is home to all life. It is also used to symbolize Hinduism itself which branches out in all directions, draws from many roots, but stems from one great trunk.

olerance, patience and generosity: trees are considered symbolic of these qualities. They allow their many gifts to be taken and used year after year. Their growth is slow and steady, creating an environment of peace and calm. They bear all difficulties, like severe cold and scorching heat, without complaint. In this way trees provide Hindus with an example to follow in their lives.

Vrindavan

Vrindavan is the name given to a sacred town on the Yamuna River and its surrounding forest in Northern India. It is considered a living symbol of Hindu environmental values and has been a place of yatra (pilgrimage) and worship for thousands of years. Over three million people visit it each year, worshipping in its many temples, bathing in the river and walking through the sacred groves (woods). It was where Krishna lived as a cowherd. His love and worship of nature have always had a strong influence on Hindu attitudes to the environment.

A story is told of how **Kaliya** the serpent entered the Yamuna River, poisoning its waters and killing the trees along its banks. Krishna wrestled with the serpent and restored the area to its original state. Sadly, in the 20th century, that beauty has again been spoilt. The River Yamuna has become polluted from the sewers and factories of Delhi. Many of the sacred groves and forests have been destroyed and animals that depended on them have disappeared. In 1991, The World Wide Fund for Nature, in partnership with the local community, began the Vrindavan Forests Revival to protect and restore Vrindavan to its former glory. This is done through fund-raising and sponsorship, involving schools and community groups. In 1992, the people of Leicester set up Friends of Vrindavan as a national charity to support this work.

Krishna is often pictured in Vrindavan, where he lived among the cowherds and charmed the **gopis** (cowgirls). Krishna is sometimes called **Gopal** (protector of the cows)

The Friends of Vrindavan logo shows a peacock feather. Vrindavan was once home to many peacocks and Krishna is often shown accompanied by one

Members of the 1996 Yamuna Cycle Yatra to Vrindavan, which raised hundreds of thousands of pounds. For 20 days between 5 and 26 October, the cyclists rode down through the Himalayas and the city of Delhi in extreme temperatures, ending in Vrindavan itself

Water

Fact file

Water is an important symbol in Hinduism. Not only does it give energy to all living things, but it also has the power to cleanse and purify. It is used at special times:

- At birth a new baby is washed, then the sacred symbol of Aum is traced on its lips.
- Before worship Hindus wash or bathe, and during arti, a **lota** (small pot of water) is one of the offerings to the deity.
- At death the body is washed before being prepared for cremation.

Rivers are treated with great reverence and are symbols of the life-giving nature of God. The most sacred of these is the River Ganga, often called Mother Ganga after the goddess of that name. According to the Hindu story, Ganga came down from heaven to earth and the power of her fall was broken by the locks of Shiva's hair, which divided Ganga into seven streams.

The belief in the power of the River Ganga to wash away sins and liberate the atman (soul) leads many Hindus to make a yatra to bathe in its waters. Whenever possible, the ashes of dead relatives are taken there to be deposited and bottles containing its water are brought back home. If the ashes cannot be taken to the Ganga, they may be scattered in the sea or in the local river (see page 60).

In January 1997, 50 years after his assassination, Mahatma Gandhi's ashes were scattered by his grandson into the River Ganga

Recall and evaluate

1 Why is Vrindavan important to Hindus? (4)

2 'There's no point caring about the environment when so many people are starving in the world.' Do you agree? Give reasons to support your answer, showing you have considered more than one point of view. (6)

Animals

Hindus find heaven in earth

A zoo is facing an increase in demand for soil trodden on by elephants, from Hindus who believe such earth is holy. Dudley Zoo in the Midlands has been giving away earth trampled over by its two elephants, Flossie and Kasama, to the local Shree Krishna Temple. Elephant-keepers scoop up the earth, keeping it in containers for members to collect. The earth is then placed over images and statues of Ganesha during ceremonies.

Fact file

As Hindus believe that the soul is present in every living creature, they consider all animals worthy of respect.

'A householder should regard deer, camels, donkeys, mice, snakes, birds and bees as his sons; for what difference is there between his sons and them?' (Srimad Bhagavatam 7:14:9)

However, humans are thought to have a higher ability through knowing the difference between right and wrong and by being spiritually aware. For this reason, animals are thought to be further back than humans in the journey to moksha (see page 6). Within the animal world itself some species are considered especially holy. These include elephants, monkeys, snakes and, in particular, cows. Many deities are shown accompanied by their respective animals. Examples include the following.

- Shiva (who destroys and recreates), with his mount Nandi, a white bull.
- Indra (the deity connected with conquest and domination), mounted on his elephant who is a sign of royalty and power, and used in many festivals.
- Ganesha (the deity who removes obstacles), with his lowly companion the rat.
- Durga (the female principle of universal energy in the universe), riding a powerful lion or tiger.

 **Get talking**

- What special qualities have you come across in pets or animals you have met or read about?

Gita is showing her friend Anna some photos of her recent trip to her grandparents in Delhi, India.

Gita: These were taken just as we were entering the city. I had plenty of time because, as you can see, there was a bit of a hold up! And you think you've got problems with the M6!

Anna: (looking at photo) Wow – a herd of cows! How on earth did these stray on to a main road? I shouldn't think the owners were too popular about this were they?

Gita: It may be hard for you to understand but cows are sacred to us so they are allowed to wander freely and safely anywhere.

Anna: Sacred? Do you mean you worship them?

Gita: No, we don't actually worship them, but they are very special to us. We believe that all creatures have a soul and are part of samsara (the cycle of birth, death and rebirth), so they must be treated with respect. This is why most Hindus are **vegetarians**.

Anna: But why are cows particularly special?

Gita: Well, if you stop and think about it, they're pretty amazing creatures. We can't eat grass, right? Cows eat grass and it's like a miracle really. They are able to turn it into all the things we need to keep us going: milk – and from that we get cheese, butter, yogurt and ghee – the butter-oil we cook with. So you can see why the cow is looked on as the emblem for Mother Earth.

Anna: I see. I don't want to be sexist about this, but where do the bulls fit into all this? They can't do all that!

Gita: Oh, they're special, too. They work in the fields, ploughing and pulling the machinery that gives us our grain and vegetables. So you see, between the two of them they provide us with the perfect, balanced diet.

Anna: OK, but you could argue that by killing them, you are providing people with meat. Surely that's important too?

Gita: It would give us a few meals, sure, but if they lived they would be able to plant and reap enough to feed hundreds of people for years. Did you know that over 34 million animals are slaughtered every year in Britain alone? Cows are such beautiful creatures. Imagine something like a state-of-the-art car being made with all its intricate design features and then immediately demolished for scrap metal.

Anna: I take it that brother of yours shares all these views?

Gita: Yes, he does and with his name you'd hardly expect otherwise. Gopal means protector of cows'!

Anna: Why is that?

Gita: It was one of Krishna's names. He himself took on the role of a cowherd boy.

Anna: Well, I shall certainly look at cows differently from now on.

Get talking

- **How would you respond to Gita's reasons for being a vegetarian?**

Cow protection

Hindus' reverence for all life and their teaching on ahimsa (see page 50) mean that many of them believe that animals should be able to live out their natural life span. For this reason, most Hindus are vegetarian. As cows are particularly revered, special sanctuaries called goshallas exist for them. These were revived in 1921 by Gandhi, who believed that because cows give so much, it is vital that Hindus protect them and set an example for the rest of the world. He said, *'In its finer or spiritual sense, the term "cow protection" means the protection of every living creature.'* There are many cow protection schemes among Hindus in India and around the world.

Adopt a cow

In 1996, in order to stop the spread of the cow disease BSE (Bovine Spongiform Encephalopathy), known as Mad Cows' Disease, the Department of Health ruled that large numbers of cattle must be killed. Partly in response to this, a scheme was developed at Bhaktivedanta Manor, which would give people the opportunity to adopt a cow. This involves donating an amount of money towards the care of a cow for a month, year or a lifetime. In return, participants receive **prashad** (see page 38) in this case, sweets made from cows' milk, and a certificate and photo of their adopted cow. They are encouraged to include the photo in their home shrine and to make a pilgrimage to the goshalla once a year.

There is a goshalla at Bhaktivedanta Manor near Watford, Hertfordshire (see page 48). Cows are taken in from commercial farms to prevent them from being slaughtered and they are able to live out their days peacefully. The bullocks are used for conducted tours and for hauling wood and ploughing. The cows provide milk for the community.

Adopt your own cow

Your choice of cows

Surabi is twelve years old, and has had one calf, Krishna. She is very friendly and gives a big yield of milk.

Nandi is our youngest ox, only two months old, brown and white and good natured.

✳ ✳ ✳ ✳ ✳ ✳

VISIT
BHAKTIVEDANTA MANOR
COW PROTECTION PROJECT
MILKING AT 4.00 PM

Creative assignment

You have been asked to contribute to a school assembly called 'All God's Creatures'. Create a feature on vegetarianism, which could be included.

'ADOPT A COW' PLAN TO SAVE BSE CATTLE

Temple leaders call on Hindus to support holy fight against slaughter

Hindu leaders plan to save thousands of British cows from mass slaughter with the launch of a new 'adopt a cow' scheme.

To adopt a cow it will cost either £31 a month, £351 a year or £6,000 for life.

The scheme will give endangered cattle a home in the fields of Bhaktivedanta Manor until the threat of a mass killing has been staved off.

A mass meeting was held at the Swaminarayan Temple in Neasden, North London last Monday to form a plan to protect the cows. 'It would be far more practical to care for the cows in Britain than sending them to India,' Mr Das explained. 'There is no way so many cows can be sent over.'

The strong reaction against the slaughter stems from the Hindu belief that killing a cow, is on the same level as killing a child. Mr Das added that cows provide more than hamburgers.

Eastern Eye, 10 May 1996

SACRED: Hindus consider the cow a holy animal

MISSION: Mr Das plans to save BSE cattle

Recall, explain and evaluate

1. What is prashad? (2)

2. 'Cows provide more than hamburgers.' Explain what Hindus believe about the contribution cows make to the world. (4)

3. 'If God made the world, it's up to him to protect it.' Do you agree? Give reasons to support your view. (4)

A sadhu (holy man) living a simple life without material comforts

Fact file

Although it is recognized that people need money in order to live, the teaching of Hinduism is against the love of wealth for its own sake since it can only bring temporary satisfaction. *'Riches come now to one, now to another … and like the wheels of a chariot are ever moving.' (Rig Veda 10:117)*

Artha (economic development) is the second of the four aims of life but Hindus believe that the other three, dharma (religious duty), **kama** (regulated pleasure), and moksha (ultimate liberation) must be worked for in a balanced way. Hindus believe that life is divided into ashramas (four stages) (see page 7) and it is only when they are in the second stage as a grihastha (householder) that they should be concerned with economic development. Attachment to worldly goods (materialism) is often thought to hinder people from achieving moksha, which is why some Hindus take up the duties of sannyasa (the fourth stage) and become **sannyasins**. This involves giving up all worldly attachments of home, family and possessions and following the life of a wandering holy man.

Get talking

● In what way can material riches
  a) help to bring happiness, and
  b) destroy happiness?

Sculpture in the Children's Zoo at Regents Park commemorating Ambika Paul

Trustees of wealth

Hindus believe that they are not owners of wealth but the trustees of what God has lent them. It is considered important to help others.

Pupils, parents, teachers and friends of the Swaminarayan School in Neasden work at fund-raising for the work of their local temple

Giving as good as they get

'A foundation [was] set up by Lord Paul, one of Britain's most successful Indian entrepreneurs and 23rd richest individual. In the mid-1960s, Swarj Paul came to London in search of leukemia treatment for his daughter, Ambika. Before she died they spent many happy hours together at London Zoo. In gratitude, he gave £1 million towards the children's zoo redevelopment and as a further memorial to his daughter he later set up the Ambika Paul Foundation, which gave £798,000 to children's causes, health and education.

He sees wealth from a Hindu perspective. 'I have never considered that it belongs to me. I am its trustee. If you are able to do something for people yet to come, you are really repaying something you have received. For example, if the zoo wasn't there we wouldn't have had a place to take my daughter. When I heard it was closing, I thought that God had put me in a position where I could do something.'

Sunday Times, 8 December 1996

Recall and evaluate

1 What is meant by the term 'materialism'? **(2)**

2 Why did Swarj Paul consider it important to give money to Regents Park Zoo? **(4)**

3 'Charity begins at home.' Do you agree? Give reasons to support your view showing you have considered other points of view. **(4)**

Food for life

Sharing food

Hospitality among Hindus is considered to be very important. There is an old custom that a place should be left at mealtimes for the **atithi** (unexpected guest).

According to Vedic teaching the distribution of prashad (see page 38) is a way of uniting the world. The Hare Krishna group works to put this into practice with its 'Food For Life' programme, started in 1972 by Swami Prabhupada, founder of **ISKCON**, the International Society for Krishna Consciousness (see page 48).

He ordered that no one within 16 kilometres (ten miles) of a temple should go hungry. Since then, the work of distributing food where it is needed has spread to over 60 countries around the world.

In the 1980s, an operation was set up in London in which a van was taken out to various points where homeless people congregated. Hundreds were served food every week. Further programmes were started in Bath, Bristol, Newcastle, Manchester and Glastonbury. In 1993, 'Food For Life' was also established in Dublin.

Hare Krishna Food for Life

Serving the World

The largest vegetarian food relief in the world

Hare Krishna 'Food For Life' provides up to 400 free meals a day to homeless people in London. Companionship and advice are also offered

'Here we are serving prasadam (spiritual food) in Shantipur in Bengal, India. We feed thousands of hungry people there. This was one of the most rewarding experiences of my life' (Pranavallabha das)

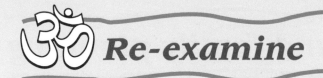

'The Earth which grows food grains, rice and barley,
On which live all types of men,
Our homage be to her,
Who mellows with the rain.'
(Artharva Veda 12:1:42)

The following questions give you a chance to re-examine the issues raised in the preceding units. Remember to look at the number of marks for each question and to develop your answer accordingly.

a What do Hindus mean when they refer to atman? **(3)**

b Why is water considered so important in Hinduism? **(5)**

c Explain how Hindus show their responsibility towards the environment. You should refer to at least two examples. **(7)**

d 'Only money can give you happiness in this world.' Do you agree? Give reasons to support your answer, showing you have considered other points of view. **(5)**

ॐ Attitudes to sex and family planning

Get talking

● The poster opposite comes from Naz Project London, a health agency which provides education on all sexual matters. To 'love safely' means different things to different people. What do you think those things are? What do you think it should mean?

Fact file

One of the four aims of life in Hinduism is kama (regulated enjoyment). This refers to sensual pleasures such as sexual intercourse within marriage. Hindus believe that sexual relationships outside marriage are wrong and that the most important purpose of sex is having children. Homosexuality is generally not accepted as it is considered to be against the natural order.

Many Hindus believe that children should not be conceived out of lust, nor should they be mere by-products of sex. After a marriage, some couples will take part in the **garbhadhan**, which is the first of the saṃskars (life-cycle rituals). At the ceremony prayers are said to purify the womb and prepare the way for the soul of a new child to enter.

Celibacy

Hindus believe that outside marriage there must be an emphasis on self-control. In **brahmacharya** (the first stage of life), **celibacy** (refraining from sexual relationships) is believed to help conserve energy for study. Similarly, those who enter the sannyasa ashram (the fourth stage of life) must strictly avoid all sexual relationships.

World AIDS Day 1996: a young girl takes part in a rally in Bombay, India, against the effects of the AIDS virus, symbolized by **Kali**, the deity associated with delivering justice

Problem page

Dear Jaya

You say you are soon to be married and have had conflicting advice about family planning. I am often asked for help on this matter and it is true that there are different views among Hindus. All I can do is to tell you what methods are available and why some people are against them for religious reasons. In the end, it is up to your own conscience to decide what is best for you.

I hope, too, that you will discuss family planning with your husband-to-be. It is really important to be able to agree on something that affects you both. So here goes …

- **The rhythm method:** this involves only having sexual intercourse at the times of your monthly cycle when you are not fertile. (Your doctor or family planning clinic will help you work this out.) Some Hindus disapprove, because they believe sex is for having children only and so should only take place at a woman's most fertile time.

- **IUD (intra-uterine device):** this is a mechanical device used internally by women. Those who are against this method of contraception consider that as it interferes with sperm, it conflicts with the teaching of ahimsa. This same view applies to the use of the condom or sheath, which can be worn by men.

- **The contraceptive pill:** many women settle for taking 'the pill'. The religious view held by some, however, is that it is wrong to take substances as this goes against the teaching in the Bhagavad Gita, which says that the body is the vehicle of the soul.

Good luck and many blessings on your marriage.

Rohini

Dear Mira

Yes, there is a way of finding out the sex of your unborn child. The method is known as amniocentesis. Some people like to know beforehand but in my experience, most prefer for it to remain a surprise. I should like to think that your interest doesn't stem from outside pressure placed on you. As you will know, traditionally, many Hindu families have had a preference for having boys. Sons are often looked on as more important as they are the inheritors of property and responsible for important religious duties. In the past, this, I'm afraid, has led to women undergoing **abortions** if they know that the unborn child is a girl.

Many Hindus see abortion as against their beliefs – except, of course, if it is on medical grounds and the mother's health is in danger. They believe that God decides when life takes place and there should be no human interference. After all, if life begins at conception (which some texts say), abortion is against the teaching of ahimsa. However, some feel less strongly about it and claim that until the fifth month of pregnancy, the embryo doesn't yet have a shape or personality. Life is very precious and it's worth remembering that three of the sixteen samskars (rites of passage) take place before birth.

Rohini

Explain and evaluate

1 Why do many Hindu women not approve of using the IUD as a form of contraception? **(2)**

2 Explain the difference between kama and karma. **(3)**

3 'There's no point in World AIDS Day – it can achieve nothing.' Do you agree? Give reasons to support your answer. **(5)**

Marriage

Wedding Invitation

Ganesha is often featured on wedding cards

BEFORE YOU TAKE MY DAUGHTER OUT, LET ME ASK YOU A FEW QUESTIONS. — WHAT DOES YOUR FATHER DO? ...

Get talking

- If you were agreeing to an **arranged marriage**, what things would you want to know about the other person?
- Which of those things would be the most important?

Fact file

Marriage is very important to Hindus and it marks the entrance into the grihastha ashrama, the second stage of life. Couples will usually have a marriage arranged by their families although both parties must agree to it. A great deal of preparation goes into making sure that the woman and man are suited to each other by considering interests, social background and caste (see page 47). To help with this, marriage bureaux are often used. Their role is to provide introductions and assist in matching people. Also, horoscopes are often consulted as a way of making sure that couples are compatible, and by predicting such things as health, prosperity and the likelihood of children.

As marriage is regarded as a sacrament where couples promise before God to make a lifelong commitment, **divorce** is not common among Hindus. Some reject it completely and many disapprove of it.

Nisha and Bharti are sisters and they are discussing Bharti's forthcoming wedding.

Nisha: Why on earth you had to choose Wimbledon Finals Day I can't imagine.

Bharti: Typical! You know perfectly I didn't have a say in it – it was down to the priest who consulted the calendar for a suitable day.

Nisha: You haven't had much say in any of it really, have you? There's no way I'm going to be dictated to when I get older. I want a love marriage – so do a lot of my Hindu friends.

Bharti: Hang on, what makes you think it isn't love with Raman and me? We weren't forced into it, as you know perfectly well. The way I look at it is if it hadn't been for Mum and Dad going to the trouble of finding someone really nice for me, I'd never have met him. As soon as I met him, I knew he was someone I could grow to love. We're on the same wave-length.

Nisha: OK, but it seems to me you don't only have to love him, but the whole of his family. I couldn't take that.

Bharti: You've been listening to too many mother-in-law jokes on the telly. There's an awful lot to get used to when you get married – running a home and everything. We shall need all the support we can get. Raman's mother did a pretty good job bringing him up so I'm sure I can learn a lot from her.

Nisha: When I meet someone, I shall want us to be independent – not so near the family so that our every move is known about and discussed. You must admit it can all get a bit closed in.

Bharti: Sometimes, maybe. But I still think the advantages outweigh the disadvantages. Think of all those babysitters we'll be able to call on! Anyway, being independent is often difficult. Let's hope you and the person you fall in love with earn good money. Not many young people can afford to set up a decent home on their own. It can be a struggle, which can often put quite a strain on a relationship. And I take it you're aware of how many love marriages break down in this country – one in three, isn't it?

Nisha: I'd still rather be responsible for my own decisions.

Ganesha is shown as having a human form with an elephant head. The large head and ears symbolise the gaining of knowledge through listening and reflecting. He is looked upon as the remover of obstacles and many Hindus worship Him before an important new step, such as marriage

Bharti: Perhaps it's because you've had more years living in England than I have, but I feel more comfortable keeping with tradition. Anyway, I shouldn't worry. Mum and Dad know what you're like and I'm sure there'll be compromises. Some of my college friends met their husbands at parties or discos organized by introduction agencies. There are quite a few of these now in London and other big cities. You can choose one that's run by people from your own caste. A lot of parents are happy with these and don't put obstacles in the way.

Nisha: I shall just have to make sure they don't put too many obstacles in my way – a few extra prayers to Ganesha, I think!

Creative assignment

Make up a leaflet called 'Taking the plunge', which contains useful information and suggestions about preparing for marriage.

Dear Tiffany

I hope your year out is going well – your German must be quite fluent by now. I'm sorry you weren't able to be here for the wedding of the year! But, as promised, here is a taste of our special day in words and pictures.

I woke up really early feeling both excited and nervous. My mother, aunt and sister helped me with my make-up. It took ages to make me look beautiful – no comment!

You won't recognize our school hall, but that's where the wedding was. We had so many guests that our local mandir wasn't big enough. The company we hired made it look really special. The canopy you can see is called a **mandap**. A temporary altar was set up with our murtis around it and a container for the **havan kund** (sacred fire).

At eleven o'clock, I set off with my parents. When we arrived, the priest was there to greet us and we had special prayers to Ganesha. We look to him as the remover of obstacles so it seemed very appropriate for this big new step in life. Near me were coconuts with a swastika marked in kumkum powder. This is a sign of God's blessing at a time of new beginnings.

Then I had to take my seat to wait for Raman and his family to arrive. All the guests were sitting round and my heart was beating pretty fast by this time. Fortunately, they were on time and my parents went to greet them and bring him to the seat next to me. Then they formally gave their consent for him to marry me. He looked brilliant – terribly serious though!

He told me later that he was terrified of getting his words wrong. He needn't have worried as the priest was really helpful guiding us through our vows. Raman made the promise to carry out his dharma (religious duties), to earn artha (money) and provide for kama (enjoyment).

The priest spoke to us about the meaning of marriage. He told us that the Sanskrit word for it is '**lagna**', which means a combination of two things mixing into one. He said that a person can't clap with one hand, but needed the help of the other. He reminded us that not only were we coming together as a couple but also that our families were being joined.

Here you see us symbolically joined by thread. My favourite words and the ones that stand out most were when Raman said: 'I am the sky, you are the earth. I am the melody, you are the hymn.' Don't you think that's beautiful? This was part of what was said as we walked around the havan kund fire in a circle. The fire is the symbol that God is present to witness our vows. This is why offerings are made to it. The most important part for us both was the **Saptapadi**, which refers to seven steps that we made to represent the idea that we will be walking together in life. Each step of the ritual stood for an aspect of our life together. We had to walk round very slowly while mantras were chanted and it was very moving in so many ways because we really felt we were making a lifelong commitment to support each other. The steps stood for food, strength, wealth, happiness, children, seasons and friendship.

When I tell you that the whole ceremony lasted three hours you will realize that there were many other rituals and mantras that also took place. So we were really quite drained at the end of it. It was wonderful though and after it was over we had a sumptuous meal in the school dining room. Needless to say it was about as different from a school dinner as you could ever expect.

Don't forget to write to my new address at Raman's parents' home.

PS Wait till you see the gold necklace Raman put on me during the ceremony – a symbol of his undying love. Who said romance is dead!

Bharti

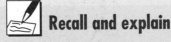

Recall and explain

1 What are the most important features in a Hindu wedding ceremony? **(6)**

2 What do you think the priest meant when he said, 'A person can't clap with one hand'? **(4)**

Home and family

The nuclear family consists of parents and their children. The extended family consists of three or more generations, including grandparents, aunts and uncles living together in the same house. In recent times, as a result of an increase in divorce and remarriage, for many people the extended family has come to mean step- and half-relatives.

Hindus, as we have seen, look on marriage as the coming together of two families, with the extended family giving support. Within this pattern, everyone has responsibilities towards one another. In this way, they are fulfiling their dharma.

Priti Shah is a 28-year-old teacher from Newcastle, who has been happily married to Sanjay Shah (also 28) for more than six years. Priti says:

I often work unsociable hours and need my own space when I come home. I like to come and go as I please without upsetting my family. I carry out my dharma by visiting my mum and dad, and by making sure that they are OK. Anyway, the house would be really cramped with more than Sanjay and myself living in it. It does mean that when we get together with the families for weddings and festivals, these occasions are really special.

There is no place like home for Pushpa Patel, the 28-year-old cleaner from Kenton, Middlesex, who would not trade in her extended family for all the money in the world. Pushpa is one of nineteen family members living in two adjacent houses. The community feeling and sense of belonging that this generates means she never feels lonely. 'We can always count on each other and no one in the family is left out.'

Because there is never a shortage of babysitters to tend to their three children, Pushpa and her husband Bhimji find plenty of time to go out and enjoy themselves. Pushpa feels the influence and guidance of elders can only benefit her children. While many have to wait for religious festivals to be part of a large family gathering, for Pushpa, every day is a Divali day.

Get talking

● Which of the two descriptions on this page is closer to your own family situation and which do you think is preferable?

Fact file

Hindus see life as a journey of ashramas towards the final goal of moksha (see page 6). In human life they believe there are four natural stages (ashramas) each with their corresponding religious duties.

- **Stage 1, Brahmacharya**
  The time of learning, often referred to as the student stage, when it is the duty to gain knowledge and to show respect towards parents and teachers.
- **Stage 2, Grihastha**
  The time of being a householder. It is considered the most important as it involves the duty to earn a living, marry, have children, support students and any other dependent family members. Traditionally, the man is looked on as the breadwinner and the one to inherit the family wealth. The woman's duties involve the management of the home and performing religious rituals. In today's society, the division of roles is changing, with many women working outside the home and following careers in addition to performing their household duties.
- **Stage 3, Vanaprastha**
  The time for retirement when the householder begins to hand over family leadership and responsibilities to the eldest son. It generally begins when the first grandchild is born. A person at this stage will have more time to attend to prayer and to give help and advice to the younger generations.
- **Stage 4, Sannyasa**
  This is an optional stage and is only adopted by a small number of Hindus (see page 33).

Recall and evaluate

1 What is meant by the terms
a) moksha and
b) ashramas?
(4)

2 What is the message about family life and values in the cartoon? **(6)**

•*When a family declines, ancient traditions are destroyed. With them are lost the spiritual foundations for life...*•
(*Bhagavad Gita 1:39*)

Growing up in the faith

There are many ways in which Hindu children learn about their beliefs, values and traditions. These include ceremonies and rituals that mark stages of their growing up, and festivals and stories told at the home shrine. Another example is seen below.

Dolls of Devotion

'Rukmini Dasi made 25 dolls for her daughter Mallika's third birthday. Each one was related to heroes from Vedic literature. She now runs a business selling dolls all over the world. She sees them as a way of strengthening children's faith. 'The dolls provide a fun way for children to become absorbed in Lord Krishna's pastimes … by having a doll, children feel that Krishna is close by.'

Fact file

Of the sixteen samskaras (rituals that mark a person's life), twelve of them take place around birth or childhood. The extent to which they are kept and the way they are celebrated varies from one tradition or jati (caste) to another (see page 47). Many families concentrate on two or three of them.

When a baby is twelve days old, the family will gather for the name-giving ceremony. In choosing a name for a child, some Hindus will have asked the priest to consult a special calendar. He will select certain syllables from which a suitable name is formed. The name will often have a special meaning (for example, the name of a god or goddess). It is then whispered into the baby's ear by the father or priest.

The **mundan** (hair-shaving ceremony) takes place between the first and third year of a child's life. It is usually performed on boys, but occasionally on girls, too. Hair-shaving symbolizes the removal of impurities from any previous life.

The **upanayana** (sacred thread ceremony) marks the beginning of adulthood for boys who belong to the three highest castes. A priest places a thread of three strands over the boy's left shoulder and under the right arm, and special mantras are recited. From this time, boys are committed to certain duties and responsibilities, which include studying the scriptures, performing puja and living a simple life, showing respect to elders.

Get talking

- What other things can children learn from playing with dolls, games and other toys?

School

Assembly at the Swaminarayan School

A large number of schools in Britain cater for particular faith groups such as Christian, Jewish, Muslim and Sikh. These schools usually follow the National Curriculum, but also teach and nurture children in their respective faiths.

The Swaminarayan School, close to the temple at Neasden, is one school of this type in Britain for Hindus. It was opened in 1991 for pupils aged from five to eighteen.

Below is a description of how Hindu beliefs, values and traditions are part of its school life.

Worship
- Daily prayers are held in assembly.
- Every classroom has a shrine area, similar to a home shrine.
- The priest comes to perform puja at important times, for example to Ganesha, remover of obstacles, at the beginning of the school year and later in the year to Saraswati, the goddess of learning.
- Visits to the temple are made several times a year.

Beliefs and traditions
- Festivals such as Divali are learned about and celebrated.
- Non-violence is promoted and vegetarianism is practised.
- Performing Arts play an important part, with teaching undertaken in Indian dance, music and drama.
- Family support and values are nurtured through the Parents, Friends and Teachers' Association (PFTA).

Values of tolerance and understanding
- Festivals from other faiths, such as Easter and Christmas, are included in assemblies.
- Teaching staff are required to have a religious belief, but it does not have to be Hindu. Pupils also do not have to be Hindu, even though the majority are.
- Self-discipline is encouraged. Pupils who have misbehaved are given time alone at the shrine to think about their actions.
- Catering staff are known by their names and not as dinner supervisors. They are given an important role in puja ceremonies.

The Community meets for lunch

Explain and evaluate

1 Explain how the Swaminarayan School aims to help develop Hindu beliefs, values and traditions. **(6)**

2 'It's a good idea for pupils of the same religion to go to the same school.' Do you agree? Give reasons, showing you have considered a range of views. **(4)**

The shrine plays an important part in everyday life

A shrine at home

"It is somewhere to recharge the batteries and find peace." (Geeta, age 48)

A shrine at the workplace

"I always associate it with my grandmother and learning about Krishna." (Ajay, age 14)

A shrine at Bhaktivedanta Manor School

"It gives me a safe sort of feeling just knowing it's there." (Meena, age 16)

"It's the only place I can be on my own. It helps to calm me down before exams." (Raj, age 15)

 Get talking

- Do you have a place where you can be on your own?
- Do you think it is a good idea? What are your reasons?

Fact file

Many Hindus' worship at home which usually features a household shrine. This may be part of a room or a small area such as a cupboard or shelf set aside for this purpose. However grand or modest it may be, it is the focal point for daily worship generally carried out by the women in the family. The shrine will feature one or more images (either murtis or pictures) of the family's chosen deity and may be decorated with flowers and sacred symbols.

Worship at the shrine is referred to as puja and it involves certain rituals using all five senses. This shows that every part of the person is involved in the worship. After a bell has been rung, the murti is bathed, dressed and offered eatables which then become sacred food (prashad). The rituals may also include the lighting of divas (lamps), the burning of incense and the recitation of prayers. At the end of the ceremony, the worshipper may respectfully eat the prashad, accepting it as God's grace.

Arti tray

Family festival

aksha Bandhan is a family festival that takes place in July or August each year. It is one of the opportunities for members of extended families to come together to reinforce their relationships. At Raksha Bandhan, girls will tie rakhis (bracelets) around the wrists of their brothers or friends as a symbol of love and friendship. The ritual can also be used for other family members to demonstrate the bonds between them. This extract from the book *A Suitable Boy* describes how different members of a family observe the festival. Veena takes a rakhi to her brother Pran, but Arun has to receive his from his sisters by post as he lives and works away from home.

Veena went in the morning to tie a rakhi around Pran's wrist. She chose a simple rakhi, a small silver flower of tinsel on a red thread. She fed him a laddu and blessed him, and received in exchange his promise of protection, five rupees and a hug …
Meanwhile the Mehra family had duly dispatched their rakhis to Calcutta. Arun had warned his sisters that anything more elaborate than a single silver thread would be impossible for him to conceal under the sleeve of his suit, and therefore entirely out of the question for him to wear to work.*

* An Indian sweet made of semolina or chick-pea flour.

Recall and explain

1 What is a rakhi and why is it worn? Why does Arun only want a plain version? **(4)**

2 Why is the home shrine considered so important by many Hindus? **(6)**

Food and fasting

McDonald's Deli in Delhi

The McDonald's food chain has opened in Delhi, India. It is the first of its 20,000 restaurants in 95 countries not to sell beef. It has invented a 'Maharaja Mac' made from mutton, and a deep-fried vegetable patty-based Mac for vegetarians. McDonald's expects to open 20 India outlets in the next three years

Get talking

● What different reasons can you think of for people making choices about what food(s) they will or will not eat?

Fact file

Hindus consider food to be very important, not just as a means of staying alive but also as a blessing from God. Food that has been offered to the deities is known as prashad (sacred food) and is shared and eaten.

Food is described in the Bhagavad Gita as fitting into three gunas (qualities) that apply to all substances. These gunas are as follows.

● **Sattva:** foods which promote good health and happiness. These include milk products, grain, pulses and vegetables.
● **Rajas:** rich or over-spiced foods, which are considered to be unhealthy because they arouse passion and can lead to disease. Some Hindus will not eat onion or garlic, for example.

● **Tamas:** food that is not fresh or that is considered unclean and thought to lead to dullness and laziness. Meat is considered by many Hindus to be tamasic.

Belief in ahimsa (see page 50) has led to many Hindus becoming lacto-vegetarian, which means they do not eat meat, fish or eggs. Because of the belief in the sacredness of the cow (see page 20), even Hindus who are less strict will not eat beef.

Fasting is important for many Hindus who see it as a way of learning self-discipline or pleasing God. It usually involves going without certain foods rather than giving up all food. Fasting times are often linked with festivals such as Janmashtami (the birthday of Krishna). Many women fast to bring God's blessing to the family.

East meets West

Most young Hindus in Britain were born there, and through school and leisure activities absorb aspects of western culture. Their own culture and religious upbringing come from their families and the mandir. Some easily adjust to being part of two cultures, but for others it can be difficult. Racism is also a serious problem, which many have to deal with. It was not until the novelist Meera Syal went to India that she realized how much easier it was to be a teenager where she was not a minority.

> *I met a whole group of young people who were comfortable with who they were and who seemed to have more freedom than some of us back in England.* (Meera Syal)

Meera believes, however, that the young people are overcoming obstacles and making their mark in British society.

The support of groups such as the National Hindu Students Forum (UK) reinforces Hindu cultural identity and promotes unity. It began in 1991 and has over 3000 students in 35 colleges. The main objectives include:

- showing a fresh and modern understanding of Hindu values
- helping teenagers to read Sanskrit
- giving voice to the views and concerns of Hindu students
- encouraging co-operation among students worldwide
- giving support and help to those who are less fortunate.

Apache Indian wows crowds in USA

Top UK bhangra singer, Apache Indian – Steve Kapur – has drawn large crowds on a visit to the United States. In New Jersey, he performed before several thousand people to help them celebrate the **Navaratri** festival. He belted out three numbers, including the highly successful 'Boom Shaka Laka'. At the same time he announced the establishment of a foundation in India to aid the poor. Royalties earned from record sales in India would be donated to the foundation, he said.

Kula Shaker wins Brit Award for Best Newcomer, 1997. The album includes the mantra Govinda Jai Jai

Recall and evaluate

1   In what ways is food considered important to Hindus? **(4)**

2   Give a detailed description of what can be seen on the Kula Shaker album cover? **(4)**

3   Why do you think the National Hindu Students Forum encourages teenagers to read Sanskrit? **(2)**

The elderly

Many elderly Hindus welcome the opportunity to go to India for pilgrimage. Here is a group from Leicestershire

There is often more time for devotion during the vanaprastha (retirement) stage

 **Get talking**

- What part have grandparents or other elderly people played in your life?
- Can you think of well-known elderly people, past or present, who have made important contributions to society?

Fact file

Dharma *of* the elderly

In Hindu tradition the stage of retirement is the third ashrama (see page 33), known as vanaprastha. At this time the responsibilities of managing the household are passed on to the adult children, leaving the elderly with time for other duties. These involve devoting themselves more to:

- service in the community and taking part in charitable activities
- playing a part in the spiritual and moral development of their grandchildren, often through story-telling
- devoting more time to studying the sacred texts and thinking about their own spiritual lives
- Going on pilgrimage.

A small number of male Hindus take up the duties of sannyasa, the fourth stage. They give up all worldly attachments and become known as sannyasins.

Sculpture at the Swaminarayan Temple at Neasden showing Shravan carrying his parents

Dharma *to* the elderly

The story of Shravan from the Ramayana

In India many years ago, there lived a young man named Shravan. His parents had grown old and blind, and they asked Shravan to accompany and guide them to the holy places of pilgrimage. This would be very tiring and involve a great deal of travelling through difficult regions. To meet the challenge and help overcome the problems, Shravan made a carrier, which looked like a set of scales, for his parents to sit in so that they could travel in comfort and with ease.

The love and devotion he showed by his actions have become a symbol of showing duty to parents. Hindus believe this is an important dharma and consider that just as children are brought into the world by their parents, so in return they should care for their parents at the end of their lives.

Care for the elderly

Traditionally, the needs of the elderly are met in the extended family. However, in Britain today, many elderly Hindus now live alone. Lifestyle patterns are changing, and often younger members of the family take up jobs and careers in areas away from the family home. Although most Hindus still take seriously their responsibilities to older family members, many of the elderly welcome the part played by organizations such as **Navjivan**, which is part of Age Concern. This is a project for elderly Asians that provides a range of services such as vegetarian lunches, transport and religious and cultural activities.

Creative assignment

If you could invite to school an elderly person you admire from the past or present, who would it be? Write a short welcome speech to introduce them and note the questions you would ask.

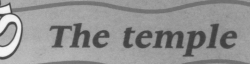

The temple

andirs (temples) in Britain are often houses and buildings that have been converted, although there are some that have been specially built (see page 44). Temples are usually opened for most of the day, but there are set times for puja. As with home worship, offerings are made to the murtis in the form of food or flowers. Shoes are removed before entering the building to signify that the ground is holy. The floor may be carpeted and worshippers will usually walk in a circle around the shrine. Many Hindus will show respect by bowing their heads and placing their palms together.

Mandirs are not only used for worship but also as centres where the young can meet and learn about their religion and where the whole community can be given support.

It is not compulsory for Hindus to worship at a mandir although many choose to do so, especially at festival times. Mandirs in Britain are usually dedicated to particular deities and will contain murtis in the most sacred area.

The importance of the mandir is illustrated in this conversation between an atheist (one who does not believe in God) and a Hindu.

Atheist: Temples have existed for many thousands of years. People have not changed. There are still wars …

Hindu (pointing to some children playing in the dirt): How many years is it since soap was produced?

Atheist: Many, many years!

Hindu: Then why are these children dirty?

Atheist: Because they don't use soap.

Hindu: Now, whose fault is it that they remain dirty?

Atheist: The kids, of course.

Hindu: Why not the soap?

Atheist: The kids have to use the soap for it to be of any use.

Hindu: This is the same principle as behind mandirs. They are not worthless. People have to use them in order to cleanse themselves. The fault lies in the people themselves, not the mandirs!

•The mandir is more important to me than when I lived in India. Here it is my community centre.'

•I like going to my mandir for festivals like Divali and Janmashtami. I'm the only Hindu in school so it makes me feel good when I see so many people worshipping like me.'

•The mandir is fun. We do lots of plays and learn dances. After Divali, I am going to learn to play the tabla.'

•Now my mother has reached the vanaprastha stage, she is spending a lot of her time helping at the mandir.'

•The holy environment helps me to focus on what is important in my life and I feel more prepared to face the day's challenges.'

Get talking

● What organizations do you belong to, both within and outside school?
● In what ways do they help you?

A community project

A branch of Hinduism followed by a large number of people is the **Swaminarayan Movement**, named after its divine leader. He and his successors taught their followers the importance of being close to their holy master and encouraged them to set up satsang sabbhas (devotional communities), where people could receive spiritual guidance and meet as a fellowship. In Britain, such communities have led to the creation of mandirs. Their construction, whether purpose-built or a conversion, is looked on as an act of devotion in itself.

A new venture in London

The sabbhas were held at a house, but as the fellowship grew in number, so too did the need for a temple in order to meet the fellowship's needs.

Step 1: Members of the fellowship met to pray regularly until a site was chosen and blessed by their Lord. The premises, an existing, empty and partially derelict building, would be bought and converted. At the satsang sabbhas, large amounts of money were pledged.

Satsang sabbha, where more than £100,000 was pledged

Step 2: A special ceremony of rituals and prayers called **bhumi puja** took place. This was performed to seek permission and receive blessings from Mother Earth in order to build the temple.

Bhumi puja being celebrated

Step 3: As the building had been vacant for fifteen years, many pigeons lived there. In accordance with Hindu teaching on ahimsa (see page 50), the birds were safely released, and hundreds of unhatched pigeon eggs were saved and kept warm for their pigeon parents to care for them.

Member of Satsang saving the little innocent birds

Step 4: The physical, mental and financial efforts used in constructing the temple are seen as **seva** (service to the Lord) and as a way to moksha (salvation). The holy leader's name is chanted as the steel is lifted into place.

Recall and explain

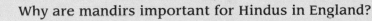

1 Why are mandirs important for Hindus in England? (5)

2 Explain how the care shown in building a mandir in England reflects the beliefs, values and traditions of Hinduism. (5)

The Swaminarayan Temple at Neasden

Prime Minister Tony Blair offering namaste greeting at the temple

'*It's so inspiring what you have all achieved. I am left speechless. Your words have touched us as much as the building – but without the building, we would never have heard your words. Thank you for your sacrifice.*'
(Richard Branson)

On the lawn, a bronze sculpture depicts Lord Krishna seated with his gopis, his women followers, shaped together in the form of an elephant. In the reception area, we abandoned our shoes to walk barefoot on polished wood floors and brightly coloured carpets made to an Indian design by an Irish company, chosen because its manufacturing system is 'environmentally friendly'.

Ruth Gledhill: *The Times*, 23 September 1995

The Swaminarayan Temple at Neasden in North London took three years to build and opened in August 1995. It is the first traditional stone and marble Hindu temple to be built in Europe and is the largest outside India. To compensate for the trees used, 2300 saplings will be sown in England and India.

As well as having a prayer hall, the mandir also has a marriage hall, a youth sports hall, crèche facilities and an exhibition centre. A large education programme deals with important issues such as health.

Get talking

● **What places or buildings have impressed or inspired you? Why?**

Divali

The temple is often the focus for the celebration of festivals. In Britain, this is especially so at Divali.

Some of the many tens of thousands of Hindus queuing to enter the Swaminarayan Temple at Neasden at Divali

Neasden

Swaminarayan serves up sweets and lights

More than 35,000 visitors passed through the doors of the Swaminarayan Temple for Divali festivities over two days last week.

However, the meaning of Divali and its religious significance was not lost amid the lights and glitter as devotees indulged in singing praises and asking blessings of God.

This involved scores of volunteers preparing prashad – blessed food – for visitors and a 100 ft-long stand in the temple's main hall was stacked with 1000 vegetarian dishes, all laid out artistically.

No less than 50,000 sachets of the sanctified prashad were handed out to devotees.

"Everyone who came to the temple to offer prayers and seek blessings was able to recharge themselves for the New Year," said Yogesh Patel, Communications Director of the Swaminarayan Temple Trust.

"This is the first year that we have celebrated Divali, so we will be looking forward to a much bigger event next time round."

Eastern Eye, 15 November 1996

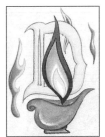

ivali is often referred to as the Festival of Light. It marks the beginning of the financial year on the Hindu calendar and is celebrated by many Hindus around the world. The word 'divali' is derived from the word 'deepavali', meaning 'row of lights', and refers to the story of Rama, an avatar of Vishnu. Rama was exiled. After fourteen years his return to his rightful place as king was celebrated, and he and his wife Sita were welcomed home by the lighting of thousands of lamps. Rama's victory, which includes the rescue of his kidnapped wife, has made him a Hindu symbol of the power of good over evil. Some Hindus associate Divali with Krishna and his capture of the demon Narakasura.

Divali lasts for five days and takes place during the darkest part of the lunar month, which falls during October or November in Britain. The association with light is marked by lighting divas (lamps) and using fireworks as part of the celebrations. The third day of the festival is when the actual new year begins. It is a time for settling debts. New clothes are bought, and cards and gifts exchanged. Special foods are eaten at family celebrations. Many Hindus will take part in worship at the mandir.

Recall, explain and evaluate

1   What is Divali?   (2)

2   Explain why Divali is considered a celebration of good over evil.   (3)

3   Why do you think people want to celebrate together instead of on their own at home? Give a range of reasons to support your views.   (5)

The Body Club strike

*There was trouble afoot at the Body Club;
President Stomach had been given the snub.
The members agreed by show of hand
It was time for them to make a stand.
They were up in arms, for while they worked
It seemed that Stomach sat and shirked.
So each took turns in having a say
Why things could not go on this way.
'We've slaved our fingers to the bone!'
'We're on our knees,' was heard their moan.
'Nose to the grindstone, shoulder to the wheel.'
'Best foot forward – it's a lousy deal!'
'It isn't fair! What's justice for?'
'We refuse to Stomach any more!'
So they went on strike to prove their point
And rested every aching joint.
But they couldn't protest for very long
For they realized things were going wrong.
In sitting it out for a week and a day
All their strength was ebbing away.
They discovered if Stomach wasn't fed
Before very long they'd all be dead.
So they called off the strike reluctantly
And made themselves a cup of tea.
Each needed the other to be nourished
So once again The Body Club flourished.*

 **Get talking**

- In what ways do you and your family members depend on each other?
- Is the system always fair to everyone?

The 'untouchables'

In addition to the four varnas and the divisions of jati within them, a fifth group of people became part of Hindu society. These people were known as the 'untouchables' and were considered to be unclean because of their birth or occupation. They had to live in poor conditions away from the rest of society and were given all the dirty tasks within the community. They were not allowed to worship in the temples or to use the village wells.

Caste hangings in India

Two lower caste youths and a fifteen-year-old upper caste girl have been publicly hanged by their own fathers in an Indian village for defying the Hindu social code barring inter-caste marriages.

Fact file

Hindus believe that all people are equal on the spiritual level. Nevertheless, there are material differences which are helpful in running society.

According to one creation story, the **Purusha-sukta**, Brahma made humans into four distinct groups from his own body. Each of the varnas (divisions) was equally important, but with a different role to play. Together they would form the whole of society and help it to run smoothly. The brahmins (priests) came from his face, the kshatriyas (soldiers and rulers) from his arms, the vaishyas (merchants and farmers) from his thighs and the shudras (labourers and craftsmen) from his feet.

Many consider that the varna system was originally based on one's natural talents and mutual support between the varnas. Later on it became hereditary (decided by birth) which has led to abuse.

Gandhi, a famous political and religious leader, spoke out against untouchability and referred to these outcastes as **Harijans**, children of God. It was largely due to him that a law was passed by the Indian government in 1948 to abolish untouchability. Further progress was made by Doctor Ambedkar, who became the champion of the oppressed classes. Himself an 'untouchable', he studied law in America and Britain. He became Law Minister in India from 1947 to 1951 and helped shape the modern Indian Constitution. Unfortunately, in practice, unequal divisions still exist.

The 'untouchables' in India today call themselves **dalits** (the oppressed) and now have voting rights. They have formed a political party and seek to improve further what is still an unfair society for many.

The Vishwa Hindu Parishad (World Council of Hindus) aims to unite Hindu society and is helping to remove divisions of caste and language.

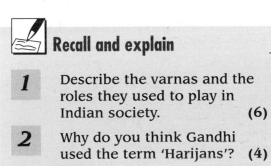

Recall and explain

1 Describe the varnas and the roles they used to play in Indian society. **(6)**

2 Why do you think Gandhi used the term 'Harijans'? **(4)**

Following the campaign to keep Bhaktivedanta Manor open for
worship, a flag was flown, showing Hanuman as a sign of victory.

● In 1973, Bhaktivedanta Manor opened at
Letchmore Heath, Hertfordshire, as the
national headquarters in Britain of
ISKCON. It stands in seventy acres of
grounds and was donated by the ex-
Beatle, George Harrison who wanted:

❛... *a real showplace for Krishna
consciousness. A place where people
could get a taste of the splendour of
devotional service to the Supreme Lord.
A tall order, to be sure, but after all, it
wasn't every day a Beatle got to go house-
hunting for God.*❜
(from *Dark Horse – The Secret Life of
George Harrison*)

● In 1993, the temple was due to close.
As a place of worship it had become the
subject of complaint from local residents
who objected to the increase in volume
and noise of traffic from visiting devotees
at weekends. Numbers were even greater
during the main festivals such as Divali
and Janmashtami, which attracted as
many as 15,000 people.

When members of the temple were
issued with orders to close, a long
campaign followed to establish their right
to keep it open.

● Programmes of fasting, prayer and
peaceful protest took place, including a
march of 36,000 campaigners showing
devotion to the cause. An appeal was
finally taken to the European Council of
Human Rights.

● In 1996, the temple was granted permission
to remain open and its members agreed to
the funding and building of a new access
road, which would help solve traffic
problems. The road, which cost £350,000,
was built in four weeks. Around 60,000
worshippers drove along it when they
attended the celebration of Krishna's
birthday soon afterwards.

ॐ Re-examine

President Mandela offering arti at the Hindu Centre at the University of Durban
'In our country, good has triumphed over evil. We are free at last to celebrate Divali without the divisions of the past'

The following questions give you a chance to re-examine the issues raised in the preceding units. Remember to look at the number of marks for each question and to develop your answers accordingly.

a Why is Divali often called a festival of 'good over evil'? **(2)**

b Explain what President Mandela is doing in the picture on this page. **(5)**

c Explain how and why the family is so important in Hinduism. **(7)**

d 'Samskaras (rites of passage) and festivals are just an excuse for having a party!' Do you agree? Give reasons to support your answers, showing you have considered more than one point of view. **(6)**

Conflict and peace

Remarkable student wins Mahatma Gandhi Award

In 1996 a new prize, the Mahatma Gandhi Award, was won by an exceptional Thames Valley University student, Rehan Siddiqui. Despite being profoundly deaf in one ear, having no hands and wearing two artificial legs, his disability has not deterred him from success.

Rehan ... has overcome numerous barriers and has been an inspiration to many other students. The award was named after Mahatma Gandhi, a person who dedicated his life to human improvement by non-violent means. The aim of the award is to reflect the goals that he strove for.

'Non-violence is not a garment to be put on and off at will. Its seat is in the heart, and it must be an inseparable part of our being.' (Mahatma Gandhi)

Get talking

● **Do you think violence is always wrong?**

Fact file

Ahimsa is usually translated as non-violence or non-injury and means 'to have reverence for all life'. It involves a mental attitude as well as not causing physical harm and is one of the yamas, the moral codes of Hinduism (see page 9).

Gandhi was a great believer in ahimsa and became famous throughout the world for his non-violent means of protest, which he referred to as **satyagraha** ('a force of truth'). He used these peaceful methods in the fight against British rule in India and other wrongs of his day. His actions involved marching and fasting, and he was occasionally imprisoned. He was supported by millions but was assassinated in 1948, six months after independence was achieved.

The **Gandhi Foundation** was set up in 1983, following the interest aroused by the film *Gandhi*. Its director, Lord Attenborough, is the Foundation's President. One of its main purposes is to show how Gandhi's teachings can be relevant to

Logo of Gandhi Foundation showing symbols of peace

many issues today. Its work includes projects dealing with non-violence training and peace education.

At the annual summer school in Oxfordshire, participants explore important issues from a Gandhian point of view

A project for world peace

Hindus' dedication to peace is seen in the words used at the end of all their prayers: 'Aum shantih, shantih, shantih.' The word 'shantih' means peace and the three kinds being prayed for are from the sufferings caused by:

(a) the mind and body

(b) natural disaster

(c) other living beings.

Recall and evaluate

1 What is meant by ahimsa? **(2)**

2 Describe one incident from this chapter showing an example of non-violent protest. **(3)**

3 Gandhi said, 'My greatest weapon is mute prayer.' What do you think he meant by this? **(5)**

Fact file

Hindus greatly value peace of mind which helps everyone perform their duties and move towards a greater spiritual understanding. They also consider it is essential to maintain a peaceful society. This was the special duty of members of the second varna, the kshatriyas, the warrior class. They were expected to be men of noble character. *'Heroism, power, determination, resourcefulness, courage in battle, generosity and leadership are the natural qualities of work for the kshatriyas.' (Bhagavad Gita 18:43).*

The word kshatriya means 'One who protects from harm'. Their duty is to protect the innocent and especially five groups within society: women, children, cows, the elderly and the brahmins (see page 7).

They would not use their weapons against innocent citizens. Even in battle there were strict codes of conduct.

In the Hindu scriptures, there are many stories of brave kshatriya kings. One of the most famous is Rama. He fought and killed the tyrant Ravana who had kidnapped his wife Sita. Hindus in Britain today celebrate this victory during the autumn festival of Dassehra.

Another example is of King Shibi who was prepared to give his own life to save that of a pigeon. He considered even animals to be citizens of the state and worthy of protection. Many Hindus question the fact some modern leaders support widespread animal slaughter and at the same time pray for world peace.

Chipko Andolan

In the hill-town of Gopeshwar in 1973
There began a peaceful protest with the hugging of a tree.
The ash trees of the forest were the dwellers' livelihood
But a company making sports gear had coveted the wood.
They paid money to the government for a licence that would win
The right to hire contractors and send the loggers in.
Though the dwellers by the forest tried to stop them coming through,
The loggers were determined for they had a job to do.
When they raised their axes to the trees to bring them to the ground
The people were protecting them by spreading arms around.
The dwellers won the battle in this brave and peaceful way,
For the loggers couldn't injure them and had to go away.
When the company persisted, choosing trees on nearby land,
The dwellers heard their neighbours' plight and went to lend a hand.
They marched and sang and beat their drums, soon joined by many more.
Arriving there they hugged the trees exactly as before.
The story didn't finish then, it only just began,
For the work continues to this day of Chipko Andolan.

Get talking

- What other ways of protesting peacefully do you know about today?
- Do you think protests should always be peaceful?

The Chipko Movement

Using Gandhi's method of satyagraha, the Chipko Andolan (the Movement to Hug), which began in 1973, has grown and flourished. It has been responsible for saving a large number of forests from being destroyed. One of its many important achievements was to win a fifteen-year ban on the commercial felling of forests in Uttar Pradesh. In 1987, it was the winner of the Right Livelihood Award (the 'green' equivalent of the Nobel Prize).

Women lead the way

The movement is, and has been from the start, mainly led by women. Many village women, who often have to walk great distances to find firewood or food for their animals, know only too well the importance of preserving the trees.

Amrita Devi

In addition to Gandhi's example, the Chipko women have undoubtedly been inspired from the start by the actions of an Indian woman called Amrita Devi who lived 300 years ago. There is a story about how she, too, led her fellow villagers in a peaceful protest to protect local trees by hugging them. The villagers were all killed in the struggle. The Indian government has honoured their sacrifice by naming their village of Khejare as India's first National Environment Memorial.

World harmony

The Hindu attitude to life is one of tolerance. Hindus do not hold the view that their particular path is the only one leading to truth and they respect that others have beliefs that are different from their own.

> *'He who loves all beings without distinction, he indeed is worshipping best his God.'*
> (Swami Vivekananda)

Swami Vivekananda (1863–1902) was born into a rich family in Calcutta and had a good education. Despite his many talents, he became more interested in religion than in worldly success. Through the influence of Sri Ramakrishna, an important guru (spiritual teacher) of that time, he began to devote his life to spiritual matters. His belief that every person is a child of God led to his teaching about harmony. At the World Fair in Chicago in 1893, Vivekananda delivered a highly successful speech to the 'Parliament of Religions'.

'Sectarianism, bigotry and its horrible descendant, fanaticism have long possessed this beautiful earth … They have filled the earth with violence.'

Until his early death at the age of 39, he continued to work for justice and harmony among people.

Concordia

Another word for harmony is concord, which is why the **Concordia** project is so named. This project is the idea of billionaire Srichand Hinduja as a way of promoting racial harmony. The plan is for a futuristic theme park in Peterborough, central England.

A GIFT FOR THE MILLENNIUM

CONCORDIA

ALL THE WORLD'S EXPERIENCES IN ONE PLACE

> *'It will be a place where adults and children can learn more about the world around them; a place where they can realize that in the ways that really matter, other people are just like them, whatever their language and whatever the colour of their skin.'*
> (Srichand Hinduja)

Creative assignment

Write a poem or a feature called 'Harmony' to go inside the brochure for Concordia.

Suffering

Get talking

● In what ways can
  a) a good action, and
  b) a wrong action have
  a 'domino' effect on
  our own or other
  people's lives?

Fact file

Hindus believe in karma (the law of cause and effect), which means that each thought and action has a consequence. Hinduism teaches that the state of the present life is the result of actions in previous lives. The accumulated karma of previous lives is called **samchita karma**. This belief helps Hindus to understand why suffering exists. It is the result of **paapa** (sinful actions).

Agami karma means actions performed in the present life which affect the future. In this way, good actions can help reduce suffering. It is the ultimate goal of most Hindus to achieve moksha, which frees them from the unavoidable suffering of the material world.

'After attaining Me the great souls never return to this temporary world which is full of miseries because they have attained the highest perfection.' (Bhagavad Gita 8:15)

Hindus believe that choosing the right path in life will not only help achieve moksha, but will bring peace of mind. Such a path is called yoga and there are various forms.

● **Bhakti-yoga – worship and loving devotional seva (service)**

● **Jnana-yoga – knowledge and understanding through study and discipline**

● **Karma-yoga – seva, service to humanity or dedicating the fruits of one's work**

One form of yoga that has found interest with many non-Hindus who realize that the material world does not provide the answer to suffering and unhappiness is Raj-yoga (self-control and meditation).

Deepak Chopra has sold six million books, including *Seven Spiritual Laws of Success*, which have been translated into 25 languages.

Among his great admirers are actress Demi Moore and singer Michael Jackson. Chopra does not like to be called a guru, which is how many see him, because although his ideas have come from Hindu Vedic writings, they have been adapted to include ideas of his own and do not conform to orthodox Hindu teachings.

Suffering for spiritual merit

Pilgrimage often involves discomfort, as the journeying to and from the sacred places can be difficult and tiring. Many Hindus accept **tapas** (voluntary hardship) as an important part of pilgrimage in helping them on their spiritual journey.

Suffering for justice

Self-denial through fasting is sometimes seen as the right action in order to put right what is wrong.

'Serving Humanity is Serving God' is the motto of the Hindu charity SEWA International, which helps to relieve suffering

More than 500,000 people have been left homeless without food, water or shelter and hundreds have been killed by the recent cyclone in the Andrha Pradesh region of India. The poor and disadvantaged are, as usual, suffering the most and SEWA International has launched an appeal.

This campaigner is showing denial of his freedom to save the temple at Bhaktivedanta Manor

Recall, explain and evaluate

1 What do you think is the message shown in the Karma Kat cartoon? **(2)**

2 Explain the relationship between karma and moksha. **(3)**

3 'What goes around comes around. You have to believe in cause and effect to make sense of this world!' Do you agree? Give reasons to support your answers, showing you have considered more than one point of view. **(5)**

In Hinduism, accepting the world as a place where permanent happiness can be found is considered an illusion (maya). Such things as money, possessions and relationships are all temporaray.

Hindus believe that spirit is permanent and unchanging. Matter is constantly changing and therefore all material things, like our bodies, are temporary. When the external soul seeks lasting happiness in this world, it is called maya. He* becomes attached to the body and material objects. His qualities are lost and he suffers from lust, greed, anger and fear.

> *'He who lacks the vision of the atman is possessed by many fears –*
> *The fear of failure ...*
> *The fear of incurable diseases ...*
> *The fear of old age ...*
> *And the greatest of all fears –*
> *The fear of death.'*
>
> **(Vibhuti Darshan)**

Beware of darkness

It can hit you; it can hurt you –
Make you sore and what is more,
that is not what you are here for
Watch out now, take care,
beware of soft-shoe shufflers
dancing down the sidewalks,
as each unconscious sufferer
wanders aimlessly, beware of
MAYA.

(George Harrison)

The ex-Beatle George Harrison learned Hindu beliefs, values and traditions from Swami Prabhupada. This is reflected in some of his albums, including 'Living in the Material World' and 'All Things Must Pass'.

Suicide

> *'The one who tries to escape from the trials of life by committing suicide will suffer even more in the next life.' (Yajur Veda 40–43)*

Taking one's life as a means of escaping suffering is against Hindu teaching. It is believed that one should concentrate on life's goals to the end. **Suttee**, the practice of widows choosing to commit suicide by being cremated alongside their husbands, was once considered to be honourable. It was made illegal in 1829.

Euthanasia (mercy killing)

The bringing about or speeding up of another's death to relieve suffering is also against Hindu teaching. Life is thought to have been given by God and Hindus believe that it is up to Him when a life should end.

Creative assignment

Either make a collage, based on lines from songs, that shows different kinds of suffering. Use suitable pictures to illustrate it.

Or devise a game of 'Snakes and Ladders' based on the law of cause and effect.

* The term 'he' is generally used when referring to the soul. This is often preferred to the term 'it', which usually applies to matter, e.g. car, cup etc.

ॐ Death and beyond

A matter of life and death

There was once a wise man who offered a blessing to four different people passing by. They were a rich prince, a student studying the scriptures, a butcher and a religious devotee.

'May you live for a very long time because when you die you will have to suffer and pay for your selfish life of greed.'

'May your time in this life end soon so that you can enjoy your reward in the next life for the righteous way you are living now. Things could change and you might fall into temptation.'

'May you neither live nor die – it makes no difference. Your life as a slaughterer is a living hell and so it will be in the life to come. So you will suffer anyway, whether you live or die.'

'May you live or may you die. It makes no difference. Being close to God, you are always happy. As a devotee you will go on remembering God in this life and in the next.'

 **Get talking**

● **What can you learn from this story about Hindu beliefs relating to life and death?**

Fact file

'*Death is inevitable for the living; birth is inevitable for those who have died. Since these are unavoidable, you should not grieve.*' (Bhagavad Gita 2:27)

Death is seen by Hindus as natural so that the atman can continue its journey towards moksha.

'*The death of the body was fixed when it was born … so you cannot stop the natural course of the body – namely birth, old age, disease and death.*' (Swami Prabhupada)

Life and death are parts of the same journey in this world and are considered to be equally good. However, in the Vedas, some deaths (especially those which are premature), are grieved over. Many Hindus approaching death try to finish all their business. They see the time given to them coming to an end and will often spend time visiting friends and doing charity work (see page 40). They may concentrate more on their spiritual life through visiting the mandir or going on pilgrimages. Difficulties can arise for some Hindus because of changing death patterns. They are concerned when life is extended artificially in hospital or when the terminally ill are sedated, because these prevent a natural end.

It is considered important for life to run its natural course and for people to be able to concentrate their last thoughts upon God.

Wayne is working on the first section of an assignment about death rites in Hinduism. He arranges to go and talk to Michelle Golden, who cares for the dying at a hospice in London and who trains others in this kind of palliative care.

Michelle: It is part of my job to make carers aware of different religious traditions. Where I am based there are people of a wide variety of cultures. Many people don't realize that they are entitled to have their wishes carried out and so they don't always like to ask for certain things to be done.

Wayne: Are there customs that Hindus would not be allowed while they are in your care?

Michelle: Well, it wouldn't be appropriate to have a shrine for worship as they do at home. This would involve using incense or candles, which we couldn't allow as they would set off the smoke detectors and fire alarms. They are allowed to have pictures of their deities, though, and they often do.

Wayne: What sort of customs would they be allowed, then?

Michelle: Well, for instance, just before death it is a Hindu tradition for the patient to be put on the floor. The carers or nurses will, if asked, be prepared to remove the mattress from the bed for this.

Wayne: Why is this done?

Michelle: It symbolizes the importance of being close to Mother Earth.

Wayne: Does a priest come in to carry out any rituals when the person dies?

Michelle: Not necessarily at this stage. They can be carried out by family members or by carers.

Wayne: What actually takes place?

Michelle: When the death occurs, water from the River Ganga or a tulsi leaf is put in the person's mouth. Sometimes the leaf is just dipped in water to moisten the lips.

Wayne: How do you get water?

Michelle: The family will often provide it, but we do keep a supply ourselves. Hindus believe that bodies should be cremated and many take the ashes of their deceased relatives to the River Ganga to be scattered. When we know this is happening, we ask them to bring back water for us to use for other people.

Wayne: What if a family can't go to India themselves?

Michelle: There is no time limit, so the family will often wait until someone else is going who can take the ashes for them. The most important thing is that the ashes go to the Ganga. It is acceptable to scatter the ashes in the sea or into a river as eventually it should mix with water from the Ganga.

Wayne: What happens after the person has died?

Michelle: The body is laid out by Hindus, preferably by the family. It is then taken to be prepared for cremation at the crematorium. Ideally this should take place within 24 hours although this is not always possible.

Funeral rites

Funeral parlour in North London used by many Hindus. Around the walls are murtis and the Aum symbol

Hindu's own symbol

Bereaved Hindus will be able to replace the cross and candles with their own symbol of God in the future. Croydon council has bought a specially crafted 'Aum' for the borough's crematorium chapels.

The pattern of a Hindu funeral is based on teaching from the Vedas. Customs vary from one tradition to another and according to the time, place and circumstances. The **antyyesti** (death rituals), which accompany the last of the sixteen samskars (see page 34), allow the family to say goodbye and express their emotions. It is also believed that the rituals bring peace to the departed soul.

The ceremony is usually led by a priest with the eldest son or nearest male relative performing some of the rites. Children are often present as they are not expected to be shielded from the reality of death. The following are some of the steps taken to prepare the deceased person for cremation and are accompanied by the reciting of mantras.

- The body is brought home from the funeral parlour.
- A dipak (lamp) is lit and placed near the head. The family keeps vigil, singing prayers and hymns.
- The next of kin sits on the right side to offer pindas (balls of rice) to the departed soul. These are placed in the coffin.
- Flowers or kusha (dried grass) are used to sprinkle water over the body.
- Tulsi leaves are dipped in water from the River Ganga, some of which is then poured into the deceased person's mouth.
- A mala (wooden bead necklace) is put around the neck.

- Sandalwood paste is put on the forehead.
- Offerings of ghee are made to the havan kund (sacred fire).
- Often a flower garland will be placed around the neck or individual flowers offered as a way of saying farewell. A widow may place her tali (wedding pendant) around her husband's neck to symbolize her tie to him. The coffin is then closed.
- The body is taken to the crematorium.

'Death is not extinguishing the light but putting out the light because the dawn has come.' (Rabindranath Tagore)

Recall, explain and evaluate

1   **What are the Vedas?**   **(2)**

2   **Explain why it is important for a Hindu to place the ashes of a deceased person in the River Ganga or other flowing water.**   **(3)**

3   **'If children are going to be able to talk about death then it is important for them to attend funerals.' Do you agree? Give reasons for your views.**   **(5)**

Cremation and burial

Most Hindus are cremated after death as it is believed that cremation allows for a swift release of the soul. Sadhus and very young children are the exception to this as their bodies are considered sinless.

Gary Beckwith of City Cruises at the launch of his new pleasure boat, *Millenium of London*. His boats are also used by Hindus taking the ashes of deceased relatives to be scattered on the Thames.

A final mantra often used for the departed is: *'O Supreme light, lead us from untruth to truth; from darkness to light; from death to immortality.'*

At a later stage, the ashes of the deceased are scattered on the waters of a sea or river. Many Hindus try to have them taken to the sacred River Ganga (see page 59). There are also a number of places that are used around the British coast, such as Blackpool in the west, Scarborough in the east and Newhaven in the south.

Gary Beckwith is managing director of City Cruises in Rotherhithe, London, which runs a passenger service on the River Thames. He owns eleven boats, including a new one named *Millenium of London*, launched by the Queen in 1996. In addition to pleasure trips, Gary offers a service to Hindus so that the ashes of deceased relatives can be scattered on the Thames. *'We have people who come from as far away as Scotland. We take them out in the boat and they conduct their own ceremony. It varies a lot, but they bring whatever they need with them. Often it is just the men of the family that come out. There usually isn't a great show of grief and emotion, which I think is to do with their belief in reincarnation.'*

Remembering the dead

Each year after a person's death a ceremony known as **shraddha** takes place. It is intended to help the dead on their journey towards moksha. Pinda offerings (balls of rice) are made and the occasion is sometimes used to remember other family members who have also died.

Reincarnation

Haven't we been here before?

From the time he could talk, Lekh Pal told his family he had lived another life in another Indian village not far from their home. He could remember his former incarnation in detail, he said, and gave a vivid account of his death, which came when he was still a small boy, a year after he had caught his right hand in a fodder-chopping machine.

Lekh would hold up his own disfigured fist as evidence: he had been born with no fingers on the right hand – an extremely unusual condition. One day strangers came to the village for a wedding and Lekh immediately claimed to recognize his mother and brothers from his previous life. They, in turn, said he was the child they had lost some years before. Today he is 20 and lives a split existence, sharing his time between his two families.

In one sense, his case is extreme – few of those who believe in reincarnation actually return to the place of their former lives as he has done.

But in many other respects he is not wholly unusual. For in the West, too, people are increasingly seeking answers through reincarnation. A Gallup Poll in 1990 revealed that one in four Americans and Western Europeans believe in reincarnation, and the majority do so because of their personal experience. Since then, the numbers have swelled.

(*Daily Mail*, 27 June, 1994)

'Seems as though reincarnation is making a comeback!'

REINCARNATION
Riding a Jaguar

What value does western civilization place on a Hindu theological concept? Well, on October 3, Jaguar Corporation spent US$300,000 for single day's advertisement with this lead line: 'Reincarnation occurs when an old soul enters a new body.' Their eight-page pitch in the *Wall Street Journal* was designed by Ogilvy and Mather, one of the world's six top advertising agencies, with annual sales of over 7.6 billion dollars. Targeting the millions in America and others the world over who are aware of reincarnation, their creative design team followed an old Hindu tradition. Gods and theological concepts often 'ride' symbolically on animals. In this case, *rebirth* 'rode' man's most elegant piece of hot rod engineering, the revolutionary new $70,000 Jaguar XK8 sports car.

Jaguar's flashy logo

Hinduism Today, January 1997

Get talking

● What do you believe about life after death? Do you have reasons for your views?
● Is what you believe the same as what you would *like* to believe?

Fact file

Reincarnation, the return of the atman after death in another bodily form, is central to Hindu belief. This process is also known as transmigration and it is believed to take place over and over again from one species to another according to a person's karma (see page 9). Those who have tried to live good lives will be reborn into a better life and vice versa. When the soul is reunited with God, the cycle of repeated birth and death is stopped. It is believed that those who are spotlessly pure will reach moksha (salvation) immediately upon leaving the present body. It is believed that certain people who are thought to have lived pure lives will escape the cycle of rebirth and reach salvation immediately (see page 60).

Many Hindus choose a path in life that will bring them closer to God and nearer to moksha (see page 54).

And whoever, at the end of life, quits the body remembering Me alone, at once attains My Nature. Of this there is no doubt.
(Bhagavad Gita 8:5)

 **Creative assignment**

Design a bereavement card from one Hindu to another following the death of a family member. Use appropriate symbols and write a short message to go inside.

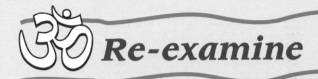

Re-examine

'After being situated in the yoga practice, and vibrating the sacred syllable Aum, the supreme combination of letters, those who think of the Supreme as they quit their bodies will certainly reach the spiritual planets.'

(Bhagavad Gita 8:14)

The following questions give you a chance to re-examine the issues raised in the preceding units. Remember to look at the number of marks for each question and to develop your answers accordingly.

a What is the symbol in the picture above and what does it mean? **(2)**

b Explain the meaning of three other symbols important in Hinduism. **(6)**

c After Indira Gandhi became prime minister of India she said, 'You cannot shake hands with a closed fist.' Explain how Hindus today try to promote peaceful living. **(6)**

d 'Hinduism isn't a religion, it's a way of life.' Do you agree? Give reasons to support your views. **(6)**

Index